Review Tales

A Book Magazine For Indie Authors

Review Tales
A Book Magazine For Indie Authors

COPYRIGHT © 2022
Review Tales Magazine
A Book Magazine for Indie Authors
This magazine may not be reproduced,
either in part or in its entirety, in any
form, by any means, without written
permission from the publisher, with the
exception of brief excerpts for purposes
of radio, television, or published review.
Although all possible means have been
taken to ensure the accuracy of the
material presented, Review Tales is not
liable for any misinterpretation,
misapplication or typographical errors.
All rights, including the right of translation,
are reserved.
Founder & Editor in Chief: S. Jeyran Main
Editor: Amy C. Shannon
Publisher: Review Tales Publishing & Editing
Services
Print & distribution: Ingram Spark
Cover Photo: Moldy-vintages
Designs: Pexels
ISBN 978-1-988680-16-3 (paperback)
ISBN 978-1-988680-17-0 (digital)
www.jeyranmain.com
For all inquiries please contact us directly.

Contribitors

A. Carina Spears: Paladin's Honor
Christina Samycia: The Journey of Discovering Inner Peace
E T McNamara: Fate's Final Destiny
Shane Wilson: The Smoke in His Eyes
Thorsten Nesch: GROLAR: HALF GRIZZLY, HALF POLAR BEAR
Danielle Dayney: When Love Sticks Around
JoDee Neathery: A Kind of Hush
Lindsay T. Dellinger: Swipe Write
Stephen Kristof: Feeling Normal Again
Stephen Murphy: The Savoy and Other Stories
Gary Orleck: Travels with Maurice
Jen Nash: The Big Power of Tiny Connections
Lawrence Berger: Instant poetry
Matt Spencer: The Night and the Land
Nathan Nish: Branching Chaos
Shruti Rao: A Wife for the Devil
Gordon Lewis: Little people
Richard DeVall: The Hypnotist's Assistant
Wendy L. Scott-Hawkins: Searching for a stranger and finding myself
J.R. Rothstein: The Alabama Black McGruder
Jennifer Lieberman: "Year of the What?"

Photo Credits from Pexels:
anastasia-belousova p.2
ahmet-polat p.2
hissetmehurriyeti
ylanite-koppens p.13
yaroslava-bondareva p.13
diana-agapova p.19
teona-swift p.24

Special thanks to:
S M Ali Boutorabi
Fatemeh Saghari Fard
Christopher R. Main
S Maysam Boutorabi
S Mohyeddin Boutorabi

Contents

Editor's Note

Summer is here, and I find myself delighted with the third issue. Look at what we have accomplished since 2016! The dedication, hard work, and determination have paid off in a very rewarding way. The articles, confessions, and reviews have been outstanding.

The third issue of Review Tales Magazine presents discussions like 'Writing Out of Anger,' 'Becoming the Author of Your Life,' and 'Writing for Personal Satisfaction.' These are topics that I know will be helpful for many authors.

For those who have worked hard to tell their stories, stayed up for hours on end re-reading and re-writing their manuscripts, and those who have looked at their work and felt lost, I want to say, dream big and be persistent.

Thank you for supporting Review Tales, and I hope you enjoy the summer edition as much as I do.

Jeyran Main

Founder & Editor-in-chief
Review Tales Magazine - Publishing & Editing Services

SUMMER 2022 | ISSUE 03

Author
Confessions

02

Contributors:

E T McNamara

A. Carina Spears

Christina Samycia

Shane Wilson

Thorsten Nesch

www.jeyranmain.com

Historical Romance

Fate's Final Destiny

E T McNamara

Writing for personal satisfaction

Writing this article caused me to reflect upon why I became an author. We all have specific reasons, but they are probably more similar than different. It's not that I entered into this field for fame or fortune. I would admit that it would be fantastic if that happened. The truth is that thousands of new books enter the market every day. An unknown author who is also an independent publisher has about as much chance of being financially successful as hitting the lottery. Yet, that did not stop me from writing anyway.

Fate's Final Destiny is my second novel. My first, The Puzzle Pieces, was done initially from boredom while locked down during the pandemic.

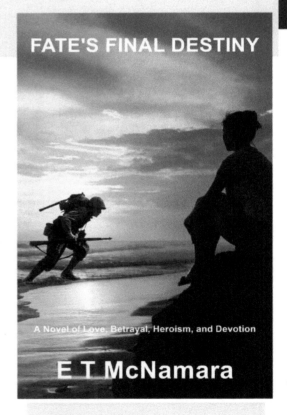

FATE'S FINAL DESTINY

A Novel of Love, Betrayal, Heroism, and Devotion

E T McNamara

Pub Date: July 7, 2021
ISBN: 13: 979-8-533485-58-6
Book Category/Genre: Historical Romance
Page Count: 371
Publisher: Self-published

It was a combination of writing a romantic mystery for my wife, a big fan of the Hallmark Channel, and a challenge to see if I could write an original, entertaining novel. Surprised and encouraged by the positive reviews, I began writing Fate's Final Destiny, a more challenging endeavor. I fully realized what an author is and why we do it during this time.

During my research for the book, I began reaching out to older citizens who lived in Goodwell, Oklahoma, where the story takes place. I wanted to get their perspective of those times to make the story and its characters authentic. I also needed to make Cindy's role and actions as a WWII Navy nurse accurate. I found and interviewed an original Naval Flight Nurse who saw action on Okinawa during WWII. It was then that I realized I had embarked upon my journey of discovery, and it was just not about writing a story. It was a life-affirming experience, and even at this stage of my life, I grew as an individual.

So, as authors, we will continue to write stories. I am currently working on my third, The Chippendale Letter. But we do it for the personal satisfaction of enlightening and inspiring our readers. If we achieve those goals, we are successful. Then, maybe we can make the world better, one page at a time.

After retiring from serving in the public sector, E T McNamara began his writing career. He attended St. John's University and Rollins College, attaining his degree in economics and post-graduate work in financial management. He has always been interested in history, and he also describes himself as a romantic who enjoys a good love story. His other interests include landscape photography, where he has received national recognition for his work. Married with three children and four grandchildren, the author believes that writing late in life is an advantage. His varied background includes being a police supervisor, a criminal investigator, a SWAT team member, a supervising court clerk, and the court official in charge of New York City's night courts. He has also spent time as a Marine reservist, a district assistant manager for a major insurance company, and a NASDAQ registered representative. These positions have provided him with real-life experiences to incorporate into his novels. The author enjoys creating a believable story and developing characters his readers can identify with. He believes that if the readers feel better after reading the story than before, he will have achieved his objective.

Fantasy

Paladin's Honor

A. Carina Spears

Writing Out of Anger

Not many people know that I often write out of anger. My entire book "Love at the End of all Things" was inspired by the scene in the television show Enterprise where they did a decontamination scene poorly. Some salve was smeared on the partially bared skin of a character just to create a sexy mood. I nearly yelled at the screen, "That's not how you do it!" It really should have been more like the decontamination scene from the X-Files: I Want To Believe movie. In that one, some bees were all sucked off one of the main characters sans one. That the MCThesuit with a collar instead of a biohazard or hazmat suit left a spot where the bee could hide and not get reclaimed by the vents. That was a believable decontamination scene.

So, I wrote a book about zombies and showed how a decontamination scene could be done right but still be sexy! Frankly, I tried to match the spice level of the novel Butterfly by Kathryn Harvey.

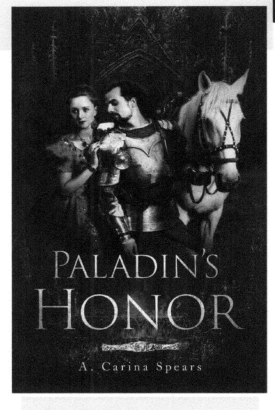

Pub Date: December 13, 2021
ISBN: 979-8-45459-418-3
Book Category/Genre: Fantasy
Page Count: 271
Publisher: White Cat Publications LLC

When I first read it, I thought the setting was terrific. When I reread it after writing Love at the End of all Things, I discovered it to be much tamer than I recalled. The politics and perils in it took more of a front seat as well.

In contrast, Paladin's Honor came from me wanting to write in a fantasy setting but finding it difficult as I started off in horror and romance first! Switching genres requires learning a different set of tools. That's why my bio quote states that "I believe that if you can master love and death, all other human experiences fall in-between those extremes." While somewhat true, it takes a lot to learn to write in other genres. Part of Paladin's Honor also came from an attempt to write erotica. That's where Theovald's origin story came from, odd as it might seem! It might see the light of day again eventually. In the meantime, for magical religious knights, check out Paladin's Honor.

A. Carina Spears has an eclectic writing style that swings like a pendulum between the polar opposites of love and death. Between these two points lies the vast totality of human existence. She believes that if you can master these two extremes, the rest will fall into place. She is a sucker for a writing dare and has appeared as Angela Barry in Haikus for Lovers: An Anthology of Love and Lust by Buttontapper Press and is featured in The Rogues Gallery anthology by Firbolg Publishing. Her latest books include Paladin's Honor from White Cat Publishing and A Keen Mind and A Phantom Song with R. J. Lloyd for the Keepers of Knowledge series in The Division of Sciences set. Having chosen the road less traveled, she aims to be like a modern-day Thomas the Rhymer, searching for fairy rings and wandering under the shadows of trees. She currently lives in Michigan with her researcher cohort and her spirit husband (who will be the first to tell you that he doesn't do parlor tricks). She enjoys reading, writing, video games, exotic cuisine, travel, and books. She'll probably like to hear about it if you can find something off-beat and quirky that she hasn't discovered yet. If you enjoy talking about books, you'll definitely have her ear.

Self-help
Psychology
Spirituality

The Journey of Discovering Inner Peace

Christina Samycia, PsyD

Becoming the Author of Your Life

As a holistic and spiritual psychologist and writer, one of my goals is to help others become the authors of their lives. We can do this by shifting out of victim-consciousness by rewriting our story, which is one of the main themes in my newly released book, The Journey of Discovering Inner Peace. In my book, I explain that we all have a story that we tell ourselves. When we were children, we created a belief system about ourselves and the world based on our childlike perspective, limited life experiences, and the beliefs of those around us. This story and its emotions become the building block of our cognitive and emotional foundation. Most of us rarely question the story about ourselves or our beliefs. We do not always understand that an inaccurate script is playing in our subconscious mind, which defines who we are, influences our lives, and motivates our decisions. This story shapes our perceptions, triggers emotional pain, and we attract experiences that reinforce it. Unless we understand this story, process our emotional pain, and rewrite it, we are trapped by it. However, we can become the authors of our lives by understanding and rewriting our stories.

When we enter into this world, we begin gathering information through the experiences we encounter.

We are receptive to our mothers, fathers', and others' feelings about us, their situations, and world views. This is the beginning of the framework of how we view ourselves and the world.

Pub Date: July 19, 2021
ISBN: 978-1-09830-416-4
Book Category/Genre: Self-help/
Psychology/Spirituality
Page Count: 135
Publisher: Suncoast Publishing

For example, if we had a narcissistic parent, we may learn to be conditionally loved. If our parents have anxiety, we might learn that we are not safe in the world because of our limited cognitive capacity during our childhood; we also create egocentric fantasies about why things happen. These speculations become the foundation of our belief systems. Although some of these beliefs may be conscious, most of this information gets stored in our subconscious minds.

As we continue to develop, we add to this framework of inaccurate belief systems and patterns of thinking and behaving, and it colors the experiences we have as we continue on our journey. These belief systems and patterns influence every aspect of our lives. They influence how we think and feel about ourselves and the world and motivate our behavior. We continue to use these inaccurate paradigms, which distort our reality because we are applying past experiences to try to explain our present reality. This is problematic because our past experiences have nothing to do with our current reality. Therefore, we do not see reality as it truly is because we use our past experiences to interpret our current reality.

The good news is that you have the power to change these belief systems on both a conscious and subconscious. You have the power to change how you appraise your reality and to determine better ways of coping and responding to these situations. You are probably not aware that you created belief systems based on your childhood experiences, which are highly inaccurate, and that you can change them at any time. It is so important to understand that many of the stress-producing beliefs about yourself and the world are not necessarily true because these beliefs were created in childhood with your childlike lenses and limited life experiences.

Although you created a story about yourself and the world, you have the power to rewrite your story and update your beliefs. Many of the beliefs we think to be true are merely opinions, which can be changed. There are very few truths that I refer to as big "T" truths. Truths with a big "T" are universal truths such as the earth is round, the sun rises in the east and sets in the west, and matter cannot be destroyed nor created, only transformed. "T" truths are absolutes, whereby everyone can agree on them. Small "t" truths are "opinions" that most of us adopt as true, usually at a very early age, because we don't challenge our belief system when we grow up. For example, the idea that "I am not lovable," "I am not good enough," etc. is a small "t" truth or opinions that we created in childhood based on our limited experiences. The "starving artist" concept is another small "t" truth. Some artists do financially struggle. However, some do not. Therefore, it is not a truth but an opinion.

As you start examining the beliefs that you hold, you may start to question these beliefs. Is that really true? A question I constantly challenge my clients with is, "Says who?" If you believe that I am not good enough, ask yourself, "Says who?" You may answer, "I don't feel good enough because I never felt like I received love and approval from my father. I was always disappointing him." Ok, but does that mean you are not good enough then or now? Why is your self-worth still measured by what your father thought then or thinks now? It doesn't have to. Just because your father said or implied some judgment of you does not make it true. You could right now decide that you are good enough, despite whatever your father may or may not have said. Again, this is an opinion of your father, not the truth. Hopefully, this article inspired you to examine some inaccurate belief systems that you may still hold that are no longer serving you so that you can start rewriting your story and become the author of your life!

Christina Samycia, PsyD, hopes to inspire and empower others to become the authors of their lives. Her life's purpose is to help evolve the planet's consciousness through her writing and guide others along their path of personal and spiritual growth. She holds a doctorate in clinical psychology, a master's degree in Kinesiology, and is the author of The Journey of Discovering Inner Peace. She has 15 years of experience as a psychologist in private practice in Chicago. She seeks to inspire and challenge individuals to discover their authentic selves and lead a more meaningful and inspired life. Her latest book, The Journey of Discovering Inner Peace, summarizes her unique approach to therapy that she has been refining for almost 15 years.

Contemporary Fantasy

THE

The Smoke in His Eyes

Shane Wilson

Emerging from Isolation

In the pre-pandemic world, I lived for public appearances. My last event before the pandemic sent all of us inside was at a staged reading of my play, The Boy Who Kissed the Rain. There is no energy like an event at a bookstore, a conference, or a literary festival. Writing is, as we know, an incredibly isolated endeavor in almost every way. As writers, we often have to go out of our way to find a meaningful conversation about the work we do. Those conversations are vital.

I always knew there was value to these interactions with readers and other writers, but I'm not sure I completely understood their true power. "Writing is a solitary act," I said when the world shut down. "What's a little more isolation?" So, I set about doing the work—writing and reading in almost complete solitude. Virtual appearances were plentiful, but they didn't hit the spot. I missed something about face-to-face interactions. I just wasn't sure what it was.

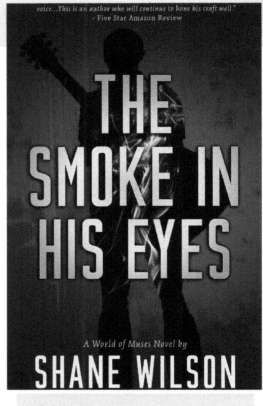

voice...This is an author who will continue to hone his craft well."
- Five Star Amazon Review

THE SMOKE IN HIS EYES

A World of Muses Novel by

SHANE WILSON

Pub Date: April 29, 2018
ISBN: 197-4-509-60-5
Book Category/Genre: Contemporary Fantasy
Page Count: 258
Publisher: GenZ Publishing

Then, as the most recent spike in cases began to come down, I was invited to speak at a literary festival three hours from home. I wasn't sure what it would be like after such a long break, but it was exactly what I needed.

I had mental fatigue—something like congestion of creative energy—but being on this new campus with students and faculty members gave me energy like I hadn't felt in two years.

Which is all to say, there is value to face-to-face interaction, especially if we tend to work in private. I feel fresh. The conversations I had about writing and publishing with people excited about books and art may be the thing I've missed most these past two years.

I hope you find a way back into the public space soon—whenever you feel safe and comfortable doing so. These opportunities provide us with new insight and fresh perspective. They get us away from the glow of the screen and replenish our creative energy—something we all need after the cruel isolation of the last few years.

Shane Wilson is a writer of contemporary fantasy stories and novels. His short fiction has appeared in The Daily Drunk, Conclave, and Door Is a Jar, among others. His novels are A Year Since the Rain (Snow Leopard Publishing, 2016) and The Smoke in His Eyes (GenZ Publishing, 2018). His third novel, The Woman with a Thousand Faces, is forthcoming from GenZ Publishing (Fall 2022).

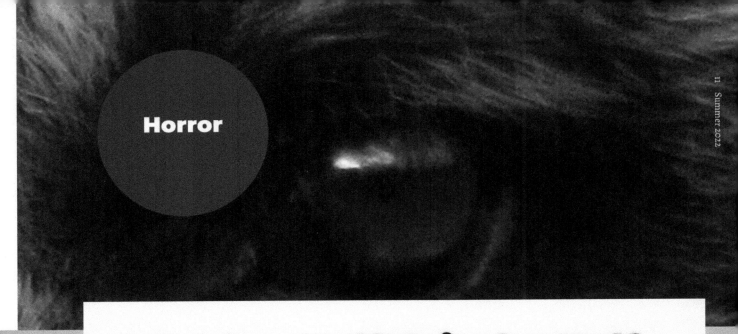

Horror

Grolar: Half Grizzly, Half Polar Bear
Thorsten Nesch

From Timeline to Novel

There are many ways to plan and write a novel. My way is to draw a timeline on one sheet of paper, then add ideas, scenes, plot, and key character developments with a pencil—so I can erase and change easily. I do this for each novel for at least a year, sometimes five years.

I never extend that sheet of paper, but I photocopy it and carry it around with me when I travel. It is a wonderful process. In the end, it looks like notes found in the front pocket of a frozen polar explorer who got lost in the ice. The entire novel fits on that letter-sized paper. I don't want more—only for grant applications, I draft a treatment. I like to keep it concise and vague at the same time in order to allow my fantasy to have room later on.

An example of a typical note read (from my horror novel GROLAR: HALF GRIZZLY, HALF POLAR BEAR): "Police/rangers arrive to help." It really just read that on my timeline.

Pub Date: May 6, 2013
ISBN: 198-0-305-77-3
Book Category/Genre: Horror
Page Count: 242
Publisher: Self-Published

I did not know how they would reach the remote gold mining camp. It turns out with a floatplane, which came with so many other twists and turns. This keeps me interested; this keeps my fantasy on its heels. Yes, some plot points have to be more specific, but I never flesh them out before I start writing the novel itself.

Visiting a scene for the first time during the writing process is the most important moment for me, largely led through the eyes and personalities of my protagonist and the other fictional characters, a moment where I have to make sure I am in the zone, one with them, much like a method actor, you can say I am a method writer. Only once you are fresh at that moment, a second visit is already a revision of their reality. I am very careful about changes at that point.

Thorsten Nesch is an award-winning author published in traditional publishing houses with more than 1,500 live readings in a dozen countries at schools, universities, book fairs, and on cruise ships.

Currently, he writes the novel SUICIDE HOTEL (received Literary Arts Grant by the Alberta Foundation for the Arts) and documents the process in multimedia blog posts on www.thorstennesch.com.

He was born in Solingen, Germany. Since 2014 in Lethbridge, Alberta, Canada.

BOOK REVIEWS

43

Review Tales is proud to have completed over 1200 book reviews. It is safe to say that we have seen our fair share of books. Our reviews have always been unbiased and constructive. We aim to help authors realize their strengths and encourage them to continue writing. 5 book reviews have been selected for this summer issue.

TO APPLY FOR A BOOK REVIEW VISIT
WWW.JEYRANMAIN.COM

BOOK REVIEW

Reviewer: Jeyran Main

LITTLE
PEOPLE

Gordon Lewis

Pub Date: March 17, 2022
ISBN: 979-8-42842-755-4
Book Category/Genre: Fantasy, Irish Folklore
Page Count: 110
Publisher: Self-Published

Little People is a children's book fantasy story set on the mythical landscape of Ireland. The story begins when Aisling and Liam are thrown into a magical world of folklore and join the little people in finding a way back. Their quest is filled with dark battles, danger, and epic adventures. Before you know it, you feel yourself attached to this book, wanting to know more.

In between the written pages, you find illustrations that add to the fantasy nature of the book. The literature is written in such a way that it grabs younger readers' minds. The characters and their personalities blend well with its Irish fairytale-style narrative.

The world-building was the most important part of the book. I paid close attention to this matter as I knew the storyline would have been the only thing that could cause the story to fall apart. I was pleased to see how it was descriptive and skillfully explained.

I recommend this book to those who like reading fantasy stories and young readers.

BOOK REVIEW

Reviewer: Jeyran Main

A WIFE FOR THE DEVIL

Shruti Rao

Pub Date: February 11, 2022
ASIN: B09R3PTSVH
Book Category/Genre: Victorian Historical Romance
Page Count: 182
Publisher: Evernight Publishing

A Wife for the Devil is a Victorian historical romance. The story begins with Elizabeth Lavoisier, a widow of 24 years of age and the illegitimate child of the Baron's younger sister and an Indian soldier. She lives with her uncle, Baron Deverill. They aren't very kind to her, and since she is penniless and her mother is being cared for by them, she has no choice but to comply with everything and the living conditions she is given.

Her cousin, Miranda, on the hand, has different plans for Elizabeth. Consumed with jealousy and just complete dislike of Elizabeth, she forces her to do as she is told, and that includes convincing the dashing Hugh Atwood to court Miranda.

The literature is written very well. You instantly get involved and feel a bond with Elizabeth. The immediate understanding of the situation prepares you for what is to happen next, and I believe that made the plot sweet and exciting to read.

I enjoyed this book as it also provided a look at the Victorian period and its social limits and expectations.

I recommend this book to those who like multicultural and interracial romance stories.

BOOK REVIEW

Reviewer: Jeyran Main

16 Summer 2022

SEARCHING FOR A STRANGER AND FINDING MYSELF

Wendy L. Scott-Hawkins

Pub Date: October 17, 2021
ISBN: 978-1-77788-250-1
Book Category/Genre: Memoir
Page Count: 308
Publisher: Self-Published

Searching for a Stranger and Finding Myself is a memoir written about Wendy growing up with a half-sibling she was really intrigued to know more about. By the time she turns thirty and after a few setbacks, only then does she begin to search for this person in question.

The entire journey for Wendy is not an easy one, but what she does find is heartwarming to read and an emotional tale to comprehend. The author describes the events very well. It is easy just to sit and read this memoir. The literature flows with her deep thoughts and makes you wonder about Wendy's strength.

What stands out most is Wendy's honesty in the telling of her story. Everything is told in steps and gradually progresses. I enjoyed how the book represented love, friendship, and passion.

I recommend this book to memoir readers.

BOOK REVIEW

Reviewer: Jeyran Main

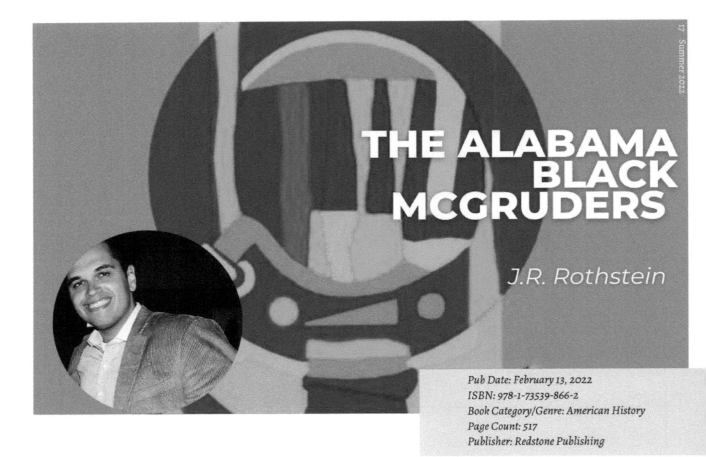

THE ALABAMA BLACK MCGRUDERS

J.R. Rothstein

Pub Date: February 13, 2022
ISBN: 978-1-73539-866-2
Book Category/Genre: American History
Page Count: 517
Publisher: Redstone Publishing

The Alabama Black McGruders is the story of Charles McGruder Sr (1829 – 1900-c), his father Ned (1795 – 1853-c), and his mother Mariah Magruder (1800 – 1880-c). Charles, the enslaved black grandson of a white slave owner, Ninian O. Magruder (1744 – 1803), was born in Alabama on the plantation of his white aunt, Eleanor Magruder Wynne (1785 – 1849,) in 1829.

Charles was sexually exploited and forced to sire hundreds of children, including 52 sons. Their story is an astonishing one, and it is all about survival. The Alabama Black McGruders continue to impact the United States culture, government, law, etc.

What you particularly enjoy besides reading the book is how it is inspiring and includes reports and testimonials at the end from McGruders living today. You also get a glimpse of the role of women during and after the civil war.

The literature is well written, and the story is told in detail. You can feel every word and be sad about what the family encountered.

I recommend this book to those who like to read about American history.

BOOK REVIEW

Reviewer: Jeyran Main

THE
HYPNOTIST'S
ASSISTANT

Richard DeVall

Pub Date: April 29, 2019
ASIN : B07RB5SZ5W
Book Category/Genre: Mystery
Page Count: 173
Publisher: Self-Published

The Hypnotist's Assistant is a Christian mystery suspense romance story about Gary and the Earl. First, you meet Earl, a fallen fireman and magician who is paralyzed, and confined to a wheelchair. You then meet Gary Crockett, a young boy who finds Earl, his neighbor, a fascinating father figure.

Earl teaches Gary how to hypnotize and other magic tricks resulting in Gary standing and walking away from his wheelchair. Gary's newfound power then takes over the story's subject, introducing all sorts of elements, including religion, racism, addiction, gender complexities, and spiritual conundrums.

The story is thought-provoking and definitely presents an entertaining and recommended read. The dialogue between the characters and the detailed descriptive nature of the storyline induced a fascinating fictional story.

I recommend this book to those who like to read an unpredictable story.

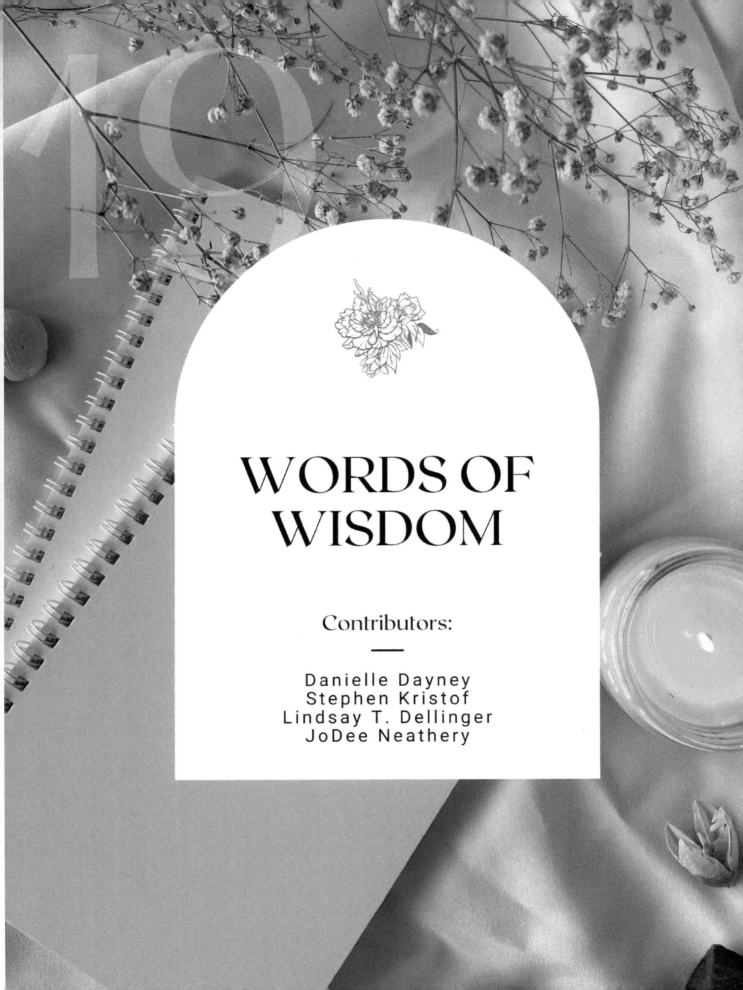

WORDS OF WISDOM

Contributors:

—

Danielle Dayney
Stephen Kristof
Lindsay T. Dellinger
JoDee Neathery

Hurry Up and Wait

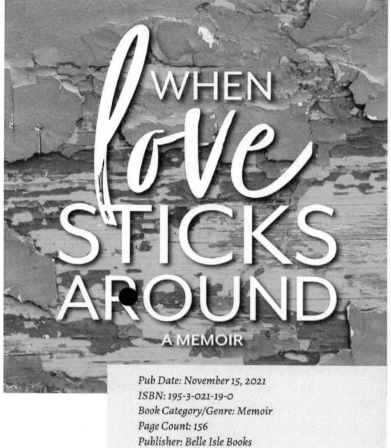

Written by Danielle Dayney

Writing, editing, and publishing take patience. In the writing process, authors have to wait for their ideas to take shape. Once their book is ready for submission, they have to wait for editors to respond. Once their book has an acceptance, they have to wait for edits, interior design, cover design, and publication date. If an author chooses to self-publish, these steps are different. Still, there is an abundance of hurrying and waiting involved.

In my experience with When Love Sticks Around, it took me two years to get it ready for a publisher's eyes. That time was devoted to asking beta readers to go through my story and contribute feedback. I tweaked, condensed, and polished. Then I prepared a list of hundreds of publishers and agents who undertook memoirs using Writer's Market, a telephone book-sized listing directory for the publishing industry. They release an amended version each year.

Once I started submitting, it took a year to get an acceptance. And after I signed the contract, it took a year to edit, proofread, and choose the cover and interior design with my project manager. I know not everyone will have the exact same experience, but with publishing, authors must always remember to "hurry up and wait."

Pub Date: November 15, 2021
ISBN: 195-3-021-19-0
Book Category/Genre: Memoir
Page Count: 156
Publisher: Belle Isle Books

I embraced the waiting, filling those weeks between each step by building my social media presence, tweaking my website, listening to marketing podcasts, and working on new writing projects. During the last few months leading up to the release of my memoir, I reached out to ARC (Advanced Review Copies) reviewers. There is always another project to work on, another lesson to be learned.

Authors shouldn't rush the writing, editing, and publishing processes. Authors should appreciate each step, take the time to study new skills, and sharpen familiar ones along the way. Trust the process. Every author's work is worth it.

Books Don't Write Themselves

Written by Stephen J. Kristof

Despite my best effort to provide some solid guidance on the subject of how to write and finish a book, there's one indisputable truth. It is often not convenient to write a book, and, more often than not, it is quite difficult!

When a writer's first manuscript is published, the title of "Author" may be justifiably assumed. Now, keep in mind that this designation has nothing whatsoever to do with the quality of the writing or how interesting it is. Then there's the issue of how many books are sold - or aren't!

Regardless, there's some degree of prestige in being able to say that one is an author; it means that one has accomplished what most others will never do, which is to complete a book and have it published. Only a minuscule proportion of people ever accomplish this feat. Last year, around 1.5 million new books were published in a world of about 7.9 billion people; less than 0.02% of everyone on earth authored a book in 2021! There are far fewer authors than there are those with doctorate degrees, so the designation is quite special.

Insofar as writing that book, there's an equation that determines the likelihood that any writer will see an idea through to a final manuscript. It goes like this, Writing Proficiency + Suitability of Idea + Available Time + Initiative + Tenacity = Probability of Completing Book.

A colleague and author gave me some advice many years ago. At the time, I had started writing three books but had not managed to finish any of them. He had completed five. While discussing my latest literary idea at a social gathering, he said, "Steve, you know, books don't write themselves."

Feeling Norma Again

A Post-Pandemic Guide to Emotional Heal

Pub Date: December 2, 2021
ISBN: 979-8-77494-798-0
Book Category/Genre: Emotional Health
Page Count: 246
Publisher: Self-published

Following that, he crowed about waking each morning at 4 to begin writing before moving on to his regular day job at 9. Embarrassed by my lack of initiative, I made a resolution to follow his schedule. It lasted exactly three days until my regular job and family life began to suffer from lack of sleep.

Several years later, after "retiring" from my regular day job, I finally finished writing and publishing my first title. Before that, I chose other priorities. In other words, I lived my life and designated my time as I saw fit. Did I miss anything by not becoming an author sooner? I'll never know. But I know that I'm happy with the time I invested in my family and professional life.

Anyone can start writing a book. Finishing it is another story. Our decisions and priorities have consequences. In the end, you are in charge of establishing those priorities.

Not One for The Rat Race

Written by Lindsay T. Dellinger

Pub Date: January 25, 2022
ISBN: 979-8-98543-970-0
Book Category/Genre: Memoir / Dating, Love, & Relationships
Page Count: 315
Publisher: Self-published

I don't know many people who would give up a comfortable six-figure income to pursue their passion. In fact, I can count them using one hand. Ever since I sat down to a casual wine tasting in Paso Robles' Tin City during Memorial Day weekend 2019 and Stanley Barrios of Top Winery told me the story of how he went from the boardroom to the barrel room, trading his corporate 9-5 for his appreciation and love for wine, the trajectory of my life changed.

I knew there had to be more out there, something beyond Disney's demands, my boss' unrealistic expectations, and stuffy offices full of unpleasant individuals. In other words, I no longer wanted to be a part of the rat race.

The wheels were turning. It began with the wheels on a 1992 International Bluebird school bus that my partner and I purchased in March 2021. We've since been converting it into a tiny home because we realized that being tied to a mortgage and a location just wasn't right for our nomadic souls. This past September, I quit my corporate fashion job as an Art Director to pursue my passion for writing. While I may not be making that pretty paycheck with benefits any longer, I've never felt freer and happier in all my life.

Growing up, my mother would tell everyone that I would be a writer someday. Unfortunately, she's no longer alive to see it all become a reality, but I like to believe that she's proud and smiling wherever she is.

I began writing my upcoming memoir, Swipe Write, in 2018 while working a 9-5. It's finally being published on January 25th, 2022, because when you decide to close one door, you have the time to discover and foster whatever is on the other side of the door that inevitably opens.

My Journey, My Challenges, My success

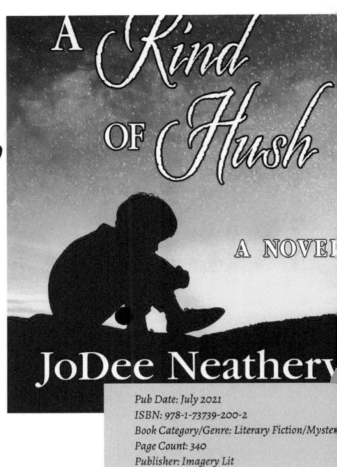

JoDee Neathery

Pub Date: July 2021
ISBN: 978-1-73739-200-2
Book Category/Genre: Literary Fiction/Mystery
Page Count: 340
Publisher: Imagery Lit

Written by JoDee Neathery

Henry Ford said, "Airplanes take off against the wind, not with it," which is a perfect analogy for writing a book. Visit a library, bookstore, or Amazon to see where the competition lies. As authors, it is our job to find a new way to tell an old story.

I was naïve, thinking my journey to publication without a writing pedigree to hang my self-confidence on would be seamless. After all, my grandmother instilled in me a sense of wonderment and endless possibilities. So, I dove in headfirst, sending the first fifty pages to a highly regarded person, who declared it unpublishable. I chose to do what it takes to make my dream come true or give up. Pat Conroy's words spoke volumes, "Four of the most powerful words in the English language are "tell me a story." I had one to tell.

Al Dewlen, an author of six novels, guided me down the right path. Novels without emotion are not novels. Find truth and base your story on it; you must know where you are going before beginning. Write the last scene first. He died before I could thank him for arming me with the wisdom to formulate a plan to pursue my lifelong dream.

Why did it take so long to jump into the fire, especially if authoring a novel has always been a dream?

Combine a Stage 4 Melanoma diagnosis, the support from my book club who believed in me before I did, and positive feedback on my writing from Pulitzer Prize-winning author Elizabeth Strout, on a review I published of Olive Kitteridge, I took science-fiction writer Ray Bradbury's advice, "First you jump off the cliff, and you build your wings on the way down."

After five years of writing, rewriting, hitting brick walls, and plowing through them, my debut novel, Life in a Box, was published in 2017, followed by A Kind of Hush in 2021 and Dust in the Wind in the incubator.

Never give up on your dreams!

AUTHOR INTERVIEW

Contributors:

Gary Orleck
Lawrence Berger
Matt Spencer
Jennifer Lieberman
Jen Nash
Nathan Nish

TRAVELS WITH MAURIC

An Outrageous Adventur in Europe, 196

"A simple thank you changed my l

Pub Date: April 2022
ISBN: 978-1-95685-110-6
Book Category/Genre: Memoir
Page Count: 250
Publisher: Touchpoint Press

01

Interview with Gary Orleck

When did you first realize you wanted to be a writer?

It took me 10 years to process the 10-week trip to Europe in 1968 with my friend Maurice. Once that trip of 10 lifetimes sunk in, I decided to research his family and all the rich and famous people I encountered. I gleaned a lot of information that was never privileged to anybody else by staying in touch with Maurice's sister Flora, and his college roommate, Moritz.

Moritz came to my home and spent 10 days with me, and I visited Flora 3 times in London over those 10 years. I was present when she was delivered her brand-new Red Ferrari Convertible for her divorce present from her Uncle John in NYC!

All this time, I gleaned more inside information about this highly secretive family [And they were secretive for a good reason, I might add], which really astonished me! The more I learned, the more I wanted to know. So I spent the next five years researching the family while working a full-time job. The minute I got the call from Moritz about Maurice's untimely death at 51 years old, I decided two things then and there. One- to honor my friend so that only he could understand. Second -To tell the world about this fantastic, larger-than-life person who, in a short time, taught me more about life than I ever realized there was to learn. I decided I would write a book so the world could see what I saw, not for fame or fortune but because it is a story that should be told!

02

What would you say is your interesting writing quirk?

My most interesting quirk was simply sticking to the truth. Do not embellish it in any way or manner because when you read this story, you WILL REALIZE that it must be true because nobody could make this story up!

03

Is there anything I'd like to confess about being an author?

Many things. It's lonesome as you're on your own while being an author! It's scary as only you know what is going on with your writing. It's sad when you get rejection after rejection, but you must realize Walt Disney was turned down for a loan to build Disney World, and Jaws was turned down by nine studios before Universal pictures said yes! I got discouraged many times, but numerous friends consoling got me not to quit! The good news is that - I learned an awful lot about myself in the process.

04

What was the most surprising thing that I learned while writing this book?

I learned just how fortunate that a simple "Thank You "changed my life for the better! Those two words took me on an adventure that most people will never experience, so I wanted to share it with them. I wanted people to know just how much I cherished my friendship with this once-in-a-lifetime person called Maurice. He could take over a room of two hundred people and be the center of attention! Just how much I learned about him, and he knew about me as we laid our souls bare! We honestly had a friendship that lasted even after his death while life got in the way. Even in death, he taught me about this world we live in-just how unique is that?

Gary Grew Up in Lincoln, R.I., a Blue-Collar town. Gary went to Babson University School of Business and graduated with a BSBA in 1966. He worked his way around The USA for 6 months. A year later, Gary traveled with the son of the richest man in the world, covering 19,988 miles, 12 countries, and 10 weeks.

Gary went to work at Broadway Tire Inc. and, 20 years later, bought the business.

Gary worked there for 50 years before retiring in 2016! He met and married his wife Ronna and had two beautiful children. Now he has 5 grandchildren! His love of travel remained with him, and he's been fortunate enough to have visited 75 Countries, each in a unique style all his own, using much of which he learned in my travels with Maurice in 1968.

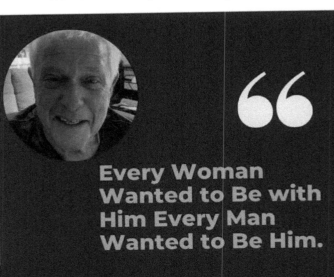

“

Every Woman Wanted to Be with Him Every Man Wanted to Be Him.

Pub Date: October 1, 2010
ISBN: 978-1-45025-552-3
Book Category/Genre: Poetry
Page Count: 52
Publisher: iUniverse

01

Interview with Lawrence Berger

When did you first realize you wanted to be a writer?

I was in the hospital in a deep depression, and I caught a fragment of the Rush Limbaugh show where he said, 'no one in America could save even $2,000.' I got mad, and my nurse helped me write what became my first book. It's old, over 5,000 copies, and was used as a college textbook. I became a writer in 1992. I worked with an agent who told me I should self-publish for my first poetry reading. I fell in love. I spent a few years going to open mics and learning how to do performance poetry. In 1999, I "went pro" and started making my living as a poet/writer.

02

What would you say is your interesting writing quirk?

I take titles from audience members and build poems on them. The technique is called Instant Poetry (Just add words!) which became the title of my book. I've literally done hundreds of poems. About 60 made it into the first edition, and that one sold out, so I did a second edition with another 80 poems. That sold out, too. So I decided to put the third edition out on a more significant publisher. I went with Universe, the biggest and best of the hybrid publishers at the time. So, it's now in its third edition.

03

How did you get your book published?

I hand-bound the books for the first edition, 20 at a time. I did a three-cities tour (Los Angeles, San Diego, and Denver). The first edition sold out at 1500 copies. I did a second edition the same way, going to readings 7 days a week and selling books. It was a lot of work, so I decided to choose a hybrid publisher for the third edition.

04

Is there anything you would like to confess about as an author?

I didn't think I'd like it so much. It's been a lot of work for a long time, but I've really enjoyed the Journey. I've met a lot of interesting characters, and each poem is a new chapter in my life.

05

As a child, what did you want to do when you grew up?

I wanted to be a Chef. My Grandfather was a master baker, and my father sold fudge. My mother didn't learn how to cook till recently. Her food was always burnt or underdone while I was growing up. So as the eldest son, I had to learn how to cook. I loved it, but I was always sick. I recently found out it was because I did a lot with salad and cruciferous vegetables. It turns out I'm highly allergic to both.

Sales Trainer. Speaker. Author. Award-Winning Poet. Laughter. Podcast Guest. Success Coach. Lawrence Richard Berger has years of experience selling everything from toner to toothpaste and applesauce to oil wells. He's written nine books, five movies, and two shorts. He wrote a TV Pilot that was written and sold within seven days. His books have been used as college texts. He's done the LASpoken, the Artwalk Alive, and the LA Times Festival of Books. He's been a working writer since 1999 and has sold over 50,000 copies of his books.

Always keep ideas brewing!

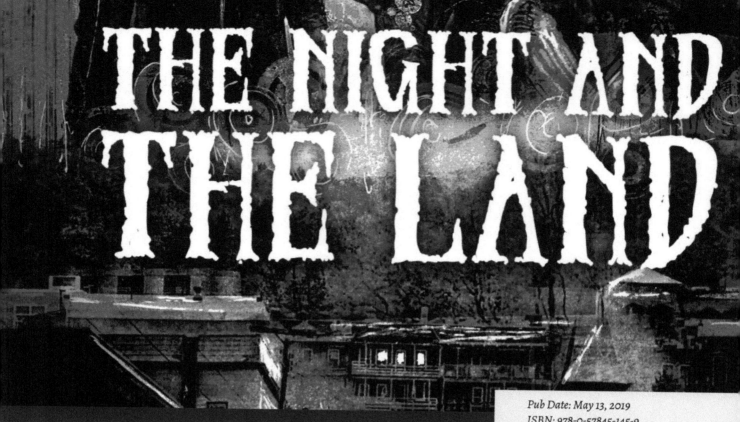

THE NIGHT AND THE LAND

Pub Date: May 13, 2019
ISBN: 978-0-57845-145-9
Book Category/Genre: Dark Fantasy/Horror
Page Count: 362
Publisher: Back Roads Carnival Books

Interview with Matt Spencer

As a child, what did you want to do when you grew up?

Before realizing that my calling in life was to be a professional storyteller, I kicked around many fanciful career ideas. As a wee lad, I wanted to be everything from a gardener/botanist to a cop at some point or other. I recall at one point wanting to grow up to be a mad scientist. Except I liked to think, had I created a monster in the lab, I'd have been nicer to him/her/them than Victor Frankenstein was to his creation and thus spared everyone all that pain and tragedy and murder. Except now, the monsters I create are the heroes and villains I write about, and I treat them with abominable cruelty, resulting in no end in pain and tragedy and murder...but hey, that's the stuff of great stories. Good thing I didn't become a mad scientist in real life, right?

What do you like to do when you're not writing?

I like to hang with friends, read books, watch movies and shows, enjoy live music, research history, train and spar in fencing and martial arts, get my drink on and give back to my community and loved ones whenever it falls to me to do so. What else is there in life?

03

What was one of the most surprising things you learned while writing this series?

I didn't expect Deschemb and its history to take over my inner creative world and subsequent career to its degree; I can tell you that!

In the early stages of the first draft of The Night and the Land, it was trying to be all sorts of unwieldy, inappropriate things at once. Like, a Stephen-King-esque small-town horror novel; a Lovecraftian cosmic horror novel; a coming-of-age story; a romance novel (yes, really); a grim, unsettlingly pessimistic deconstruction of the Joseph Campbell hero's-journey monomyth (before such pessimistic deconstructions went through their latest phase of being "cool," no less); a quirky slice-of-life narrative depicting all the colorful folks in my community, compassionately presented warts-and-all; an unfiltered exorcism of all sorts of PTSD from those past couple years, including the recent death of a close friend. The thought experiment of how cool it would be to take all the elements I loved about pulp sword-and-sorcery. The stories of Robert E. Howard and Michael Moorcock that I'd been reading voraciously t had gotten me through some of the worst times. And drop them into the reality I was seeing every day and watch how it shook out. Eventually, I somehow managed to distill all that down into what became the book's final form. There's also one character that I expected to kill off halfway through, and letting that character live wound up redefining the entire course of the rest of the trilogy.

Matt Spencer is the author of five novels, two collections, and numerous novellas and short stories. He's been a journalist, New Orleans restaurant cook, factory worker, radio DJ, and a no-good ramblin' bum. He's also a song lyricist, playwright, actor, and martial artist. He lives in Vermont with his girlfriend and two cats.

If you're going to try to make it in this business, you have to grow a thick skin.

Year of the What?

Pub Date: November 18, 2020
ISBN: 978-1-77532-682-3
Book Category/Genre: Humor, Romantic Comedy, Chick Lit
Page Count: 214
Publisher: Maple Mermaid Publishing Corporation

01

Interview with Jennifer Lieberman

What was one of the most surprising things you learned in creating your book?

I was completely surprised by how much fun it was to write this book, especially since I had already performed the story, and up until this point in my life, my main focus was writing specifically to create performance opportunities for myself. The idea of writing an entire book for the first time was daunting and intimidating; I was afraid I wasn't a good enough writer to write a book. I was blown away by how the story and characters took on lives of their own and evolved way beyond the shell of what they were able to be/do on stage. The process didn't feel effortful, and I experienced little resistance to sitting down to write; all of this was surprising.

The second big surprise was that my original title, "Year of the Sl*t," was censored from all ads on amazon and social media, pretty much killing it before it even had a chance in the marketplace. The title that packed houses in New York and won an award was considered too offensive for ads. So, I decided to re-title, rebrand, and relaunch the book under the new title "Year of the What?" This was extremely frustrating because it's a female empowerment piece, but the bots or algorithms don't understand nuance.

02

When did you first realize you wanted to be a writer?

As a child, I fantasized about being on popular TV shows like "Saved By The Bell," so I began writing myself guest roles in fan fiction at 8 years old. Eventually, those fan fiction scripts evolved into original pieces. In addition to scripts, I also enjoyed writing poetry and short stories through middle school and high school, which I still do today. I never thought I'd write books, though, yet I am.

03

How do you process and deal with negative book reviews?

No one loves to get negative feedback, but sometimes it's valuable to hear. It's what pushes us (at least me) to become better. Sure, I may bitch or cry about it in the process of digesting the comments, but it's all part of the writing (and creative) world. Not everyone will love me or my work, and I simply must accept that. I take the feedback that's useful, throw away the rest, and move forward. Learning what feedback to listen to and what to throw away is a skill I've developed over the years since everyone will have an opinion about my work, and many of those opinions will be contradicting.

Jennifer Lieberman is from Maple, Ontario, Canada, and holds a Bachelor of Arts in Philosophy from York University in Toronto. Jennifer has appeared in over thirty stages Lieberman's Award-Winning Solo Show "Year of the Slut" is now the Amazon #1 Best Selling Novel "Year of the What?" In addition to Jennifer's performance career, she has penned a number of screens and stage plays, including the wacky web-series Dumpwater Divas and the short films Leash and Details which both screened at the Festival De Cannes' Court Métrage, among other international film festivals. Other books by Jennifer include "Make Your Own Break: How To Master Your Virtual Meeting in Seven Simple Steps" and Amazon #1 Best Seller "Make Your Own Break: How To Record & Publish Your Audiobook In Seven Simple Steps."

" I'm active and outdoorsy. I love being in nature.

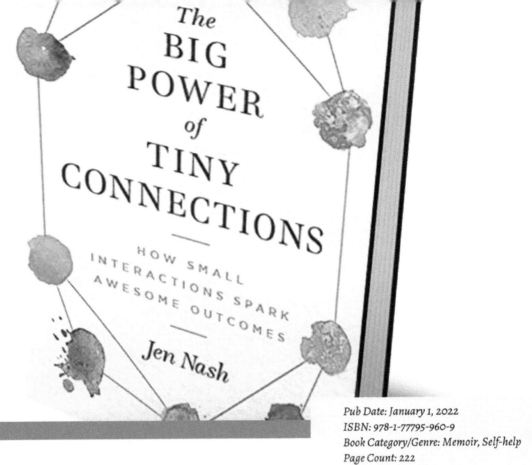

Pub Date: January 1, 2022
ISBN: 978-1-77795-960-9
Book Category/Genre: Memoir, Self-help
Page Count: 222
Publisher: Big Shift Press

Interview with Jen Nash

When did you first realize you wanted to be a writer?

I started keeping journals when I was six, despite the fact that I couldn't spell at all. I still have some of those old journals, and they're the cutest things ever. But I really knew I wanted to be a writer during my Junior year at Parsons School of Design, which is a very respected University for fashion, fine art, illustration, and communication design (CD). I was studying to be an Art Director in the CD department. When I was pouring over the award annuals, I'd get really frustrated because I'd start reading the stories (instead of looking at the winning layouts), and they'd be cut off. Design annuals only typically showcase the opening spread of an article. Somehow in that frustration, I realized I love words. The images were nice, but it was the words and headlines that really caught my attention. From then on, I switched my focus, took a tone more writing classes, and even landed a job as a financial journalist right out of university.

As a child, what did you want to do when you grew up?

I loved animals, so as a kid, I had every intention to grow up and be a vet and take great care of animals. Instead, I grew up and became an author, a speaker, and an executive coach. So, while I foster and nurture wild, gorgeous entrepreneurial spirits, I wouldn't call them animals.

How do you process and deal with negative book reviews?

I'm very fortunate that I haven't had any negative reviews of my book, but it is interesting to see how I react internally when people dislike something that's integral to my book or good friends give it four stars instead of five stars. The ego part of me is really taken aback, but I'm also a grown-up who gets you just can't take stuff like this personally. One of my exes wrote not one but two glowing reviews, then deleted both of them. If I were to get caught up in that, I wouldn't have time for anything else. Of course, different comments have absolutely rubbed me the wrong way—but I spent decades in marketing and advertising, so I know you can't please everyone. You just can't.

What do you like to do when you're not writing?

Well, considering I just wrote a book about connection, it won't come as much of a surprise when I tell you that I love spending time connecting with friends. I love trying new restaurants, being physically active, and swimming and walking or biking around amazing cities like New York, Los Angeles, or San Miguel de Allende. I'm historically a huge travel buff, but I will admit that covid put a little damper on that plus, I'm newly single, so it's taking me a minute to adjust to moving through the world solo again. Funny how you get into the rhythm of being a duet, and it takes a beat to get back to being all you, all the time!

Nonetheless, I'm finding my way, enjoying friends and new adventures, and working a lot. I'm really focused on supporting my executive coaching clients as well as growing my corporate training offerings and, of course, speaking wherever I'll make an impact.

Jen Nash grew up moving around the world. By the time she was 18, she'd moved ten times around Canada before moving to Malaysia, Hong Kong, Japan, Australia, and then the United States. It makes sense that she'd write a book called The Big Power of Tiny Connections, as all this globe-trotting gave her a sense of urgency with regard to making friends and connections. Beyond being an author, Jen is a speaker and an executive coach for HNW females, and she helps companies support employee retention by improving their culture, mental fitness, and masterful storytelling capabilities.

Get up at 5 am and write til noon... then you can handle all the stuff that life throws at you after that.

BRANCHING

CHAOS

Pub Date: July 16, 2020
ISBN: 979-8-66709-576-7
Book Category/Genre: Psychological Thriller /
Horror, Sci-fi
Page Count: 206
Publisher: Self-published

Interview with Nathan Nish

01

When did you first realize you wanted to be a writer?

I was sitting at a table in a kitchen, writing my fifth or sixth short story, when I was twelve. I really liked Goosebumps and thought, "I wanna do what that guy does." I don't know if anyone else in my second-grade class read the R.L. Stine interview printed in the newspaper that year, but I'm sure it's all they heard from me for a week.

02

What do you like to do when you're not writing?

I've really liked video games since 1990 when I was 2. I still play a lot of them. But, as an adult, I try to remember playing video games doesn't get the writing done (yet.)

03

What was one of the most surprising things you learned in creating your book?

As horrible as living day-to-day can sometimes look, I learned it was worth my time to add more fun to reality.

04

How do you schedule your life when you're writing?

I did the "prioritize writing first" thing with this book, except for a break a little over halfway through writing, to focus on college full-time. After graduating, I would write for 2-8 hours a day and repeat the process while putting in the time to revise and edit for another 2-8 hours a day, usually 6-7 days a week for most of 2016-2019. Writing during the pandemic has made me shift my priorities a little. I took a break for about a year, starting in the summer of 2020. These days, I just write for a few hours a week while editing the audiobook for Branching Chaos to have some variety.

05

Where did you get your information or idea for your book?

Talking to many different people about a lot of various conspiracy theories, I noticed there were sentiments gaining traction about certain conspiracies. People with vastly different views talked about the same conspiracies, with their own slightly different perspectives of events, and the differing versions interested me. I was also watching many horror movies; American Horror Story had just released their first season and was very popular. I loved the idea of doing a sort of anthology, and Black Mirror became popular in the U.S. while I was in college. Reading some kind of writers one finds difficult to discuss in casual conversation probably had a lot to do with the ideas for the book, too.

Nathan Nish started life in a small town before moving away from it with his parents within weeks to a desert. After wandering around a college elsewhere for almost ten years, he obtained an Associate degree in sociology. He wrote most of the Branching Chaos series during his time teaching. Between writing projects, he enjoys making music and listening to more music. Otherwise, a lot of his free time goes to watching horror movies, most of which are not scary.

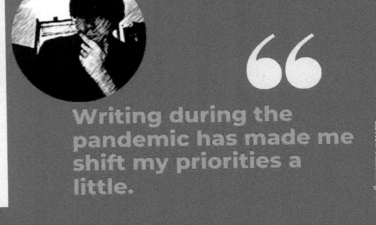

66

Writing during the pandemic has made me shift my priorities a little.

STARRED BOOK

The Savoy and Other Stories - Stephen Murphy

A warm-up comedian with a career crisis…
A lonely woman discovers a message attached to a red balloon…
A cinema strangely stuck in time…
Here are 17 stories about people and connecting. Details on the edge of the day to day. The power of a quiet moment. The strength of enduring life. The menace of the unexplained. Welcome. Enter the Savoy.

Pub Date: March 21, 2022
ISBN: 199-9-663-04-7
Book Category/Genre: Short Stories
Page Count: 144
Publisher: Blackgate Media

Stephen is married with two children, lives in Lancashire, UK, and teaches film production at Salford University while running a successful film festival (www.penninefilm.com). He has self-published a film reference book, 'Keeping it Long: Why filmmakers use the long-take and its relevance to a modern cinema audience,' A novel, 'Something Worth Finding' is his first book of short stories.

CONTRIBUTING AUTHORS

Summer 2022 Edition

A. CARINA SPEARS

Paladin's Honor

CHRISTINA SAMYCIA, PSYD

The Journey of Discovering Inner Peace

E.T MCNAMARA

Fate's Final Destiny

SHANE WILSON

The Smoke in His Eyes

THORSTEN NESCH

GROLAR: HALF GRIZZLY, HALF POLAR BEAR

DANIELLE DAYNEY

When Love Sticks Around

JODEE NEATHERY

A Kind of Hush

LINDSAY TAYLOR DELLINGER

Swipe Write

STEPHEN J. KRISTOF'S

Feeling Normal Again

STEPHEN MURPHY

The Savoy and Other Stories

GARY ORLECK

Travels with Maurice

JEN NASH

The Big Power of Tiny Connections

LAWRENCE R. BERGER

Instant Poetry

MATT SPENCER

The Night and the Land

NATHAN NISH

Branching Chaos

SHRUTI RAO

A Wife for the Devil

GORDON LEWIS

Little People

RICHARD DEVALL

The Hypnotist's Assistant

WENDY L. SCOTT-HAWKINS

Searching For a Stranger and
Finding Myself

J.R. ROTHSTEIN

The Alabama
Black McGruders

JENNIFER LIEBERMAN

"Year of the What?"

9 781988 680163